# TIM JEFFS ART
## Animal Sketches
# Saltwater Fish

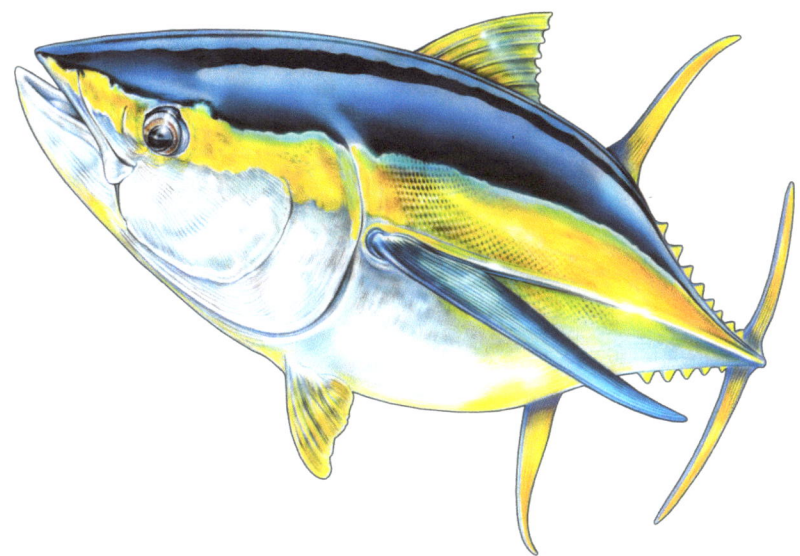

**Coloring Book**

# Saltwater Reflections

**I have always had a fascination with sea life.** Becoming a scuba diver at the young age of 14 and having the chance to go open water diving many times throughout my life has brought me to respect and view in amazement the creatures that live beneath the ocean waves. This coloring book brings together many of the saltwater fish I have drawn over the years. From the mighty Blue Marlin to the tiny Google Eye, this compilation of 20 drawings will exact any ocean angler or enthusiast to pick up a coloring pencil and have fun!

**Tim Jeffs**
Wildlife Artist

**For Jane, Jenna and Harrison**

Dedicated to all of the wonderful colorists who have supported my art and made my drawings more beautiful with their colors, and all the precious creatures that we live among.

A special thank you to Jo Warren and Karl Jennings for all of their continued support.

© Copyright 2021 Tim Jeffs Art

All rights reserved. No part of this publication may be reproduced or distributed in any form without the prior written permission of Tim Jeffs Art.

Tim Jeffs Art

376 East Madison Avenue, Dumont, NJ 07628

# Saltwater Fish Index

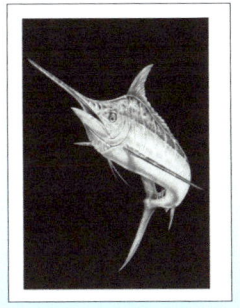
Blue Marlin 1

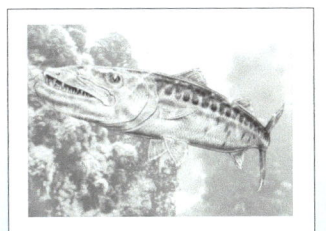
Great Barracuda 5

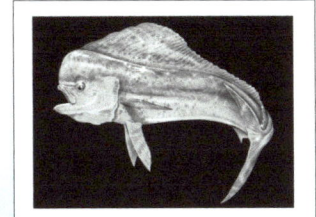
Mahi Mahi 9

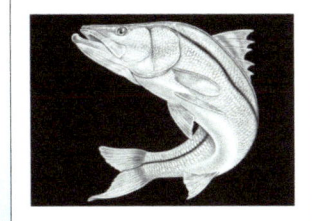
Snook 13

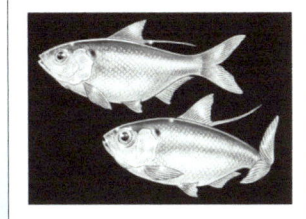
Threadfin Shad 17

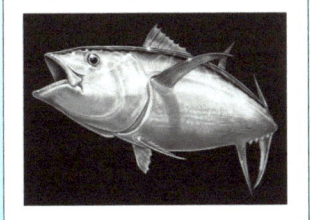
Bluefin Tuna 2

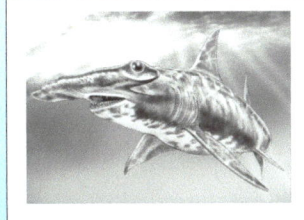
Great Hammerhead Shark 6

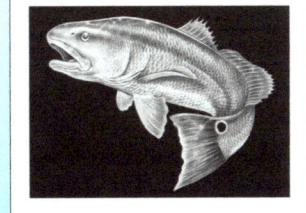
Red Drum 10

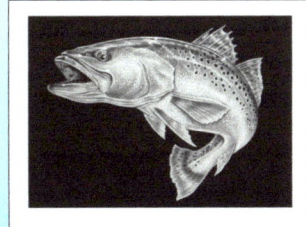
Speckled Trout 14

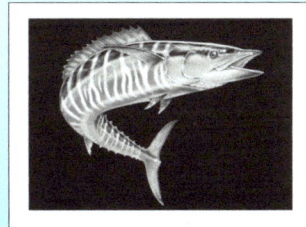
Wahoo 18

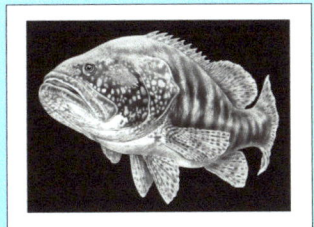
Goliath Grouper 3

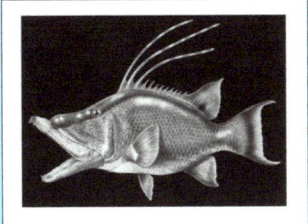
Hogfish 7

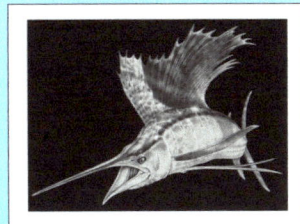
Sailfish 11

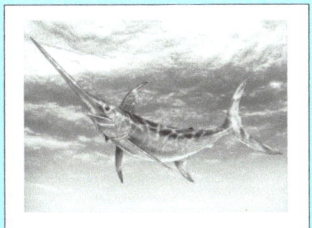
Swordfish 15

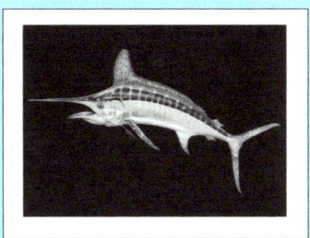
White Marlin 19

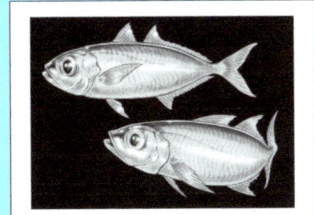
Google Eye 4

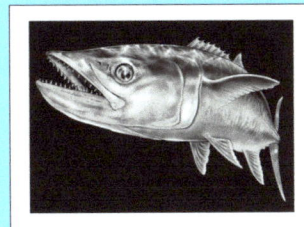
King Mackerel 8

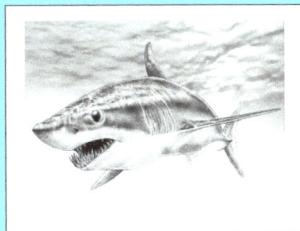
Shortfin Mako Shark 12

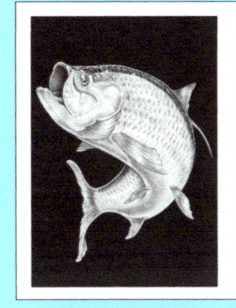
Tarpon 16

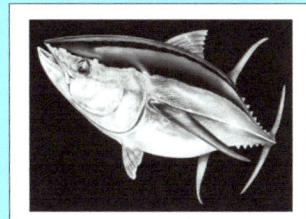
Yellowfin Tuna 20

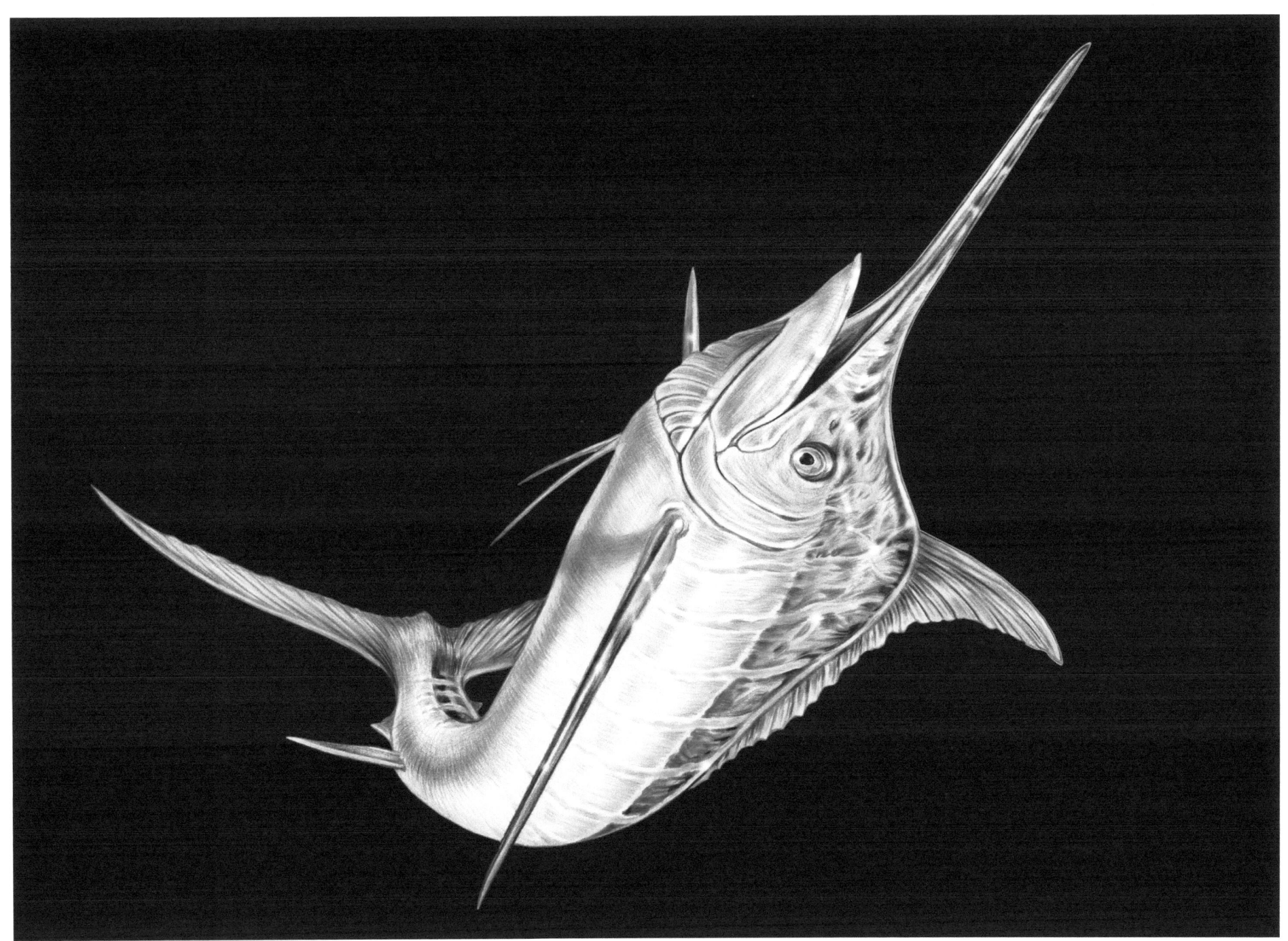

Blue Marlin

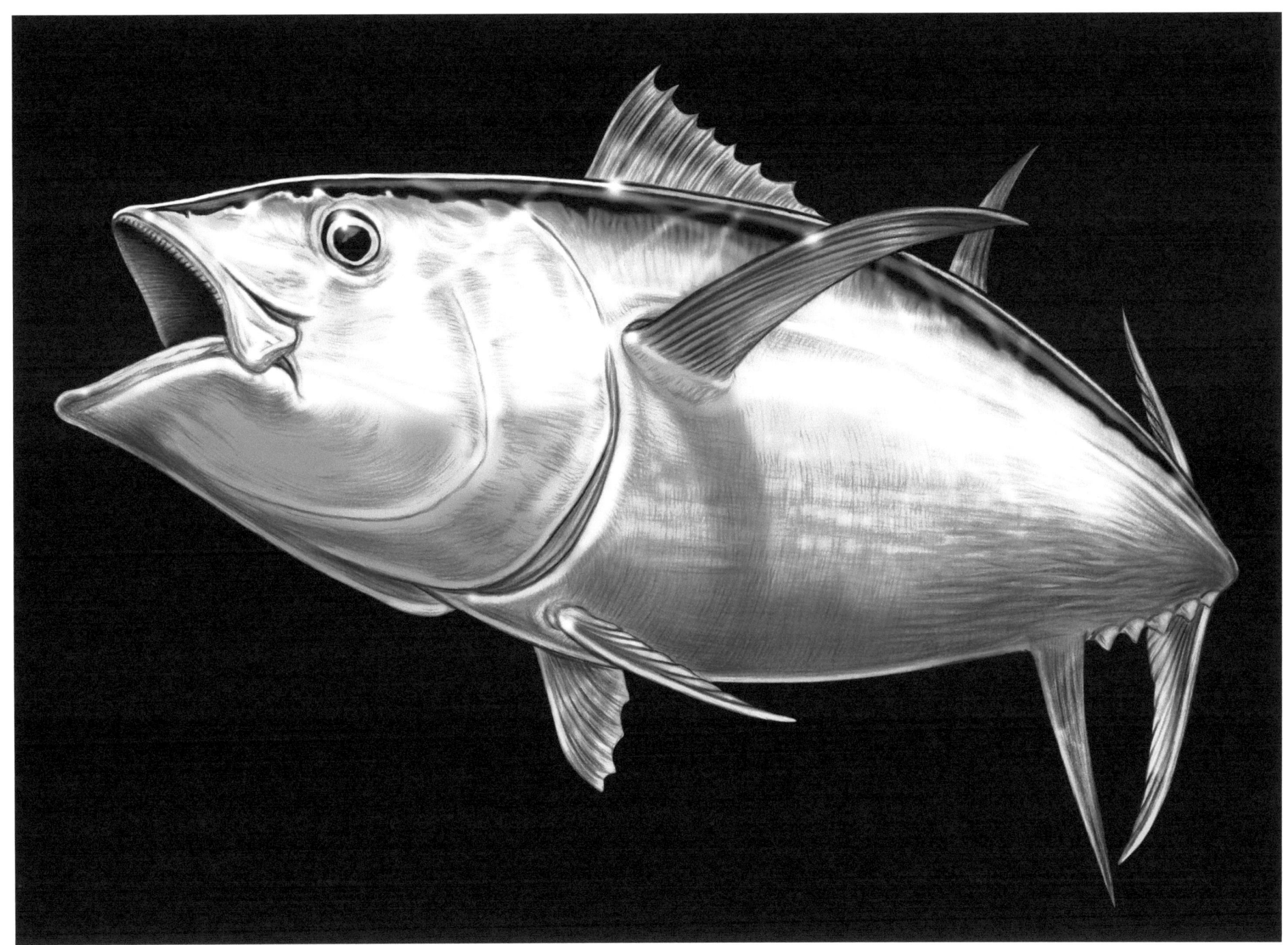

Bluefin Tuna

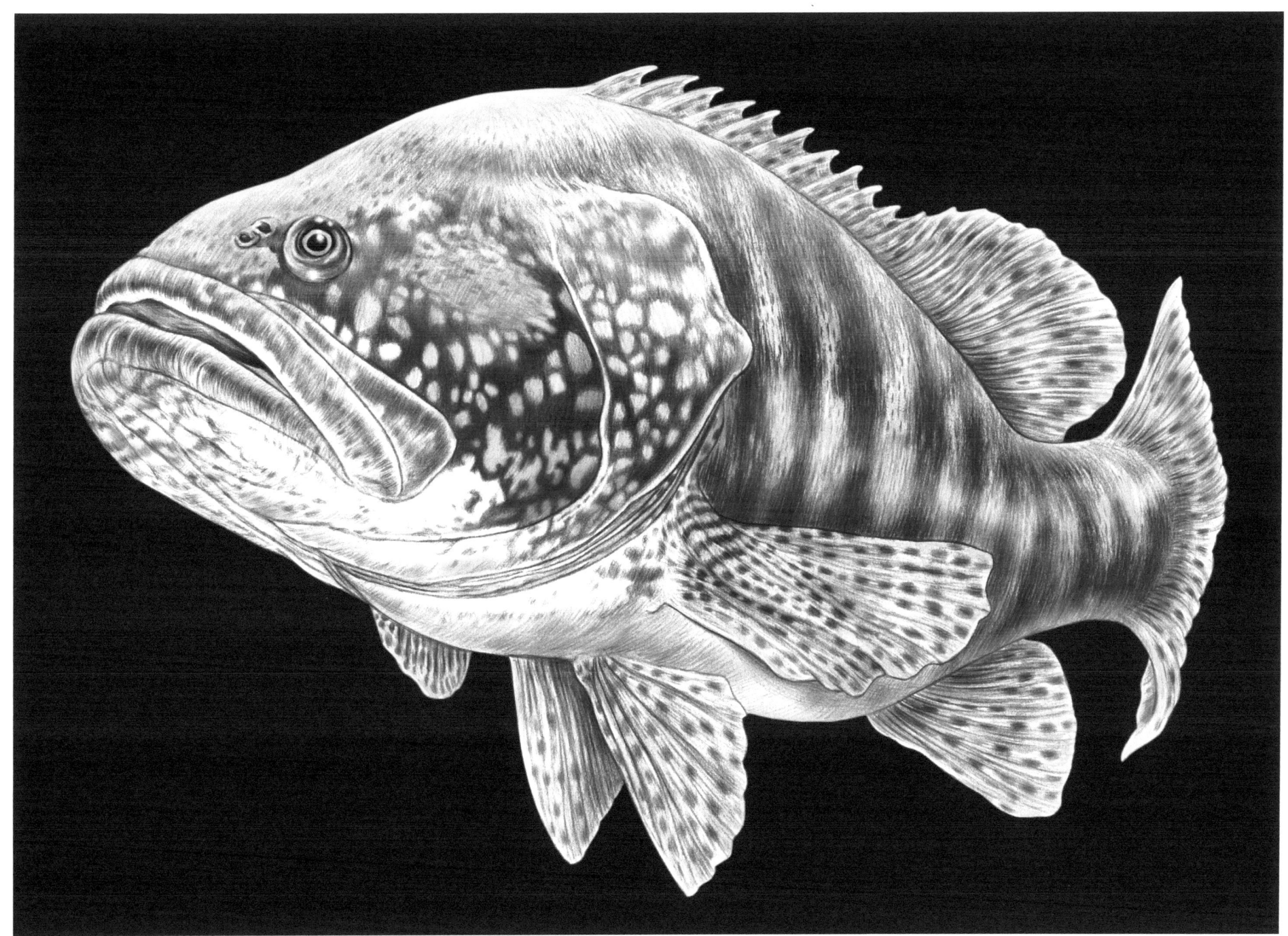
Goliath Grouper

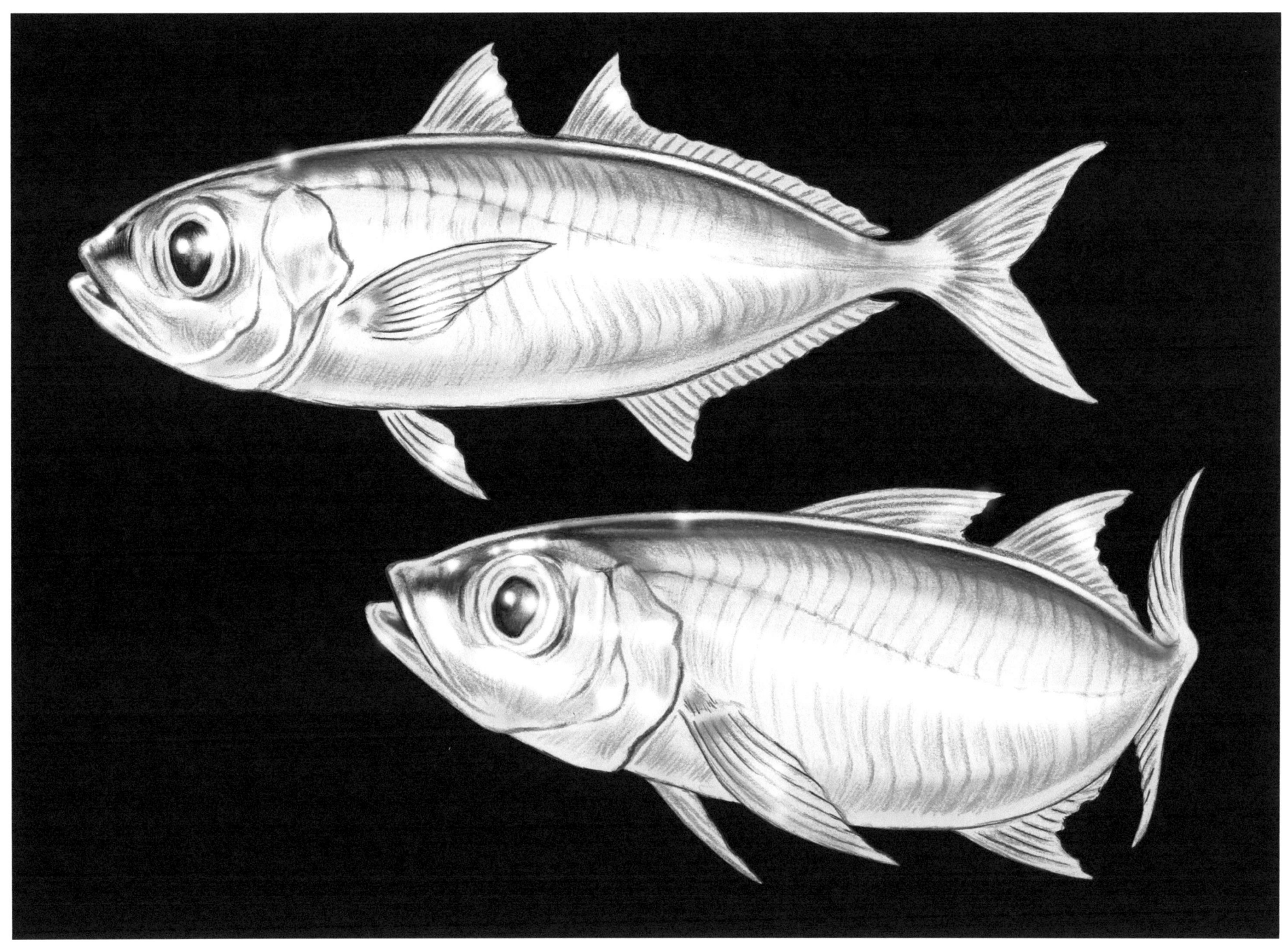

Google Eye

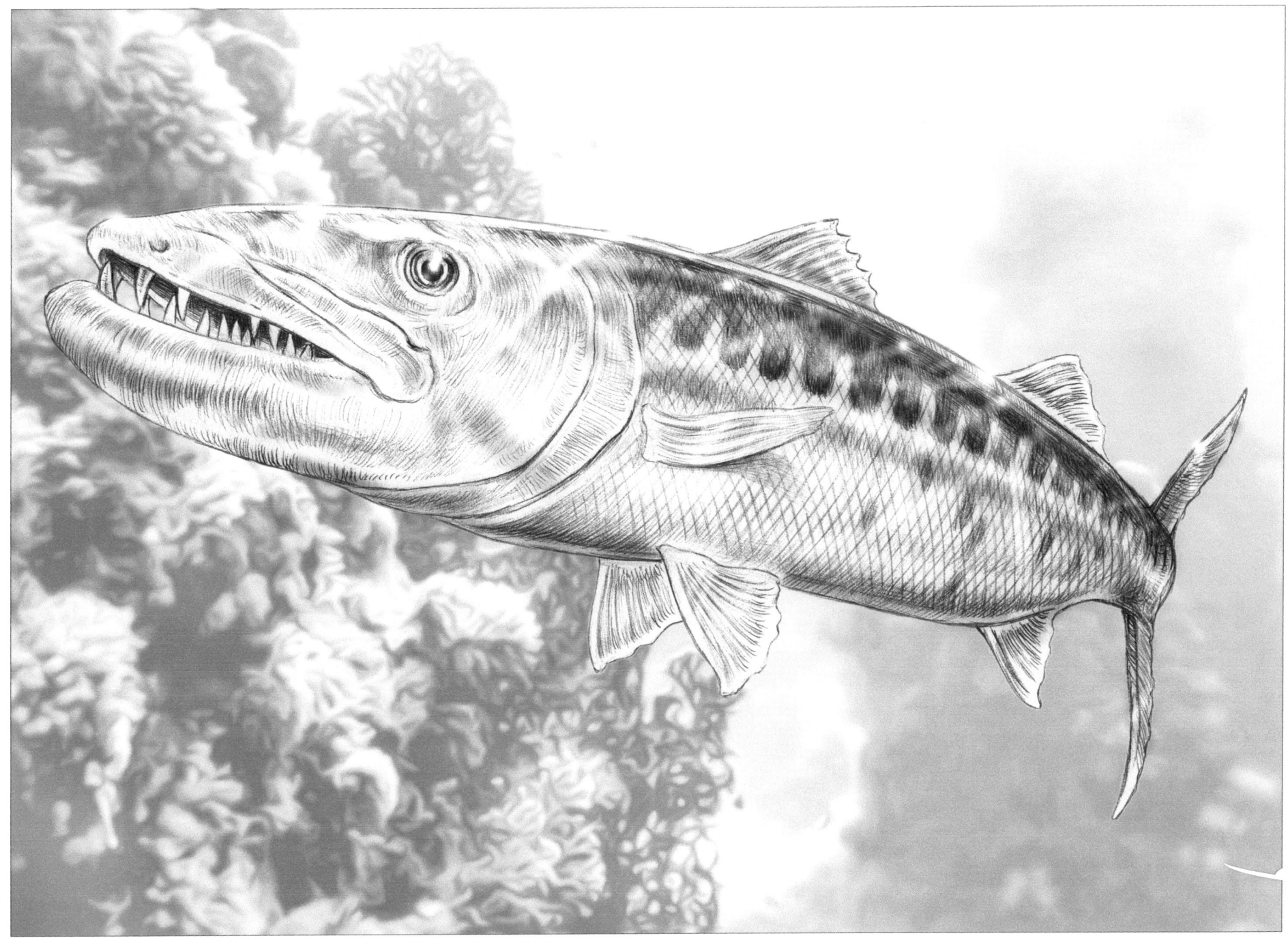
Great Barracuda

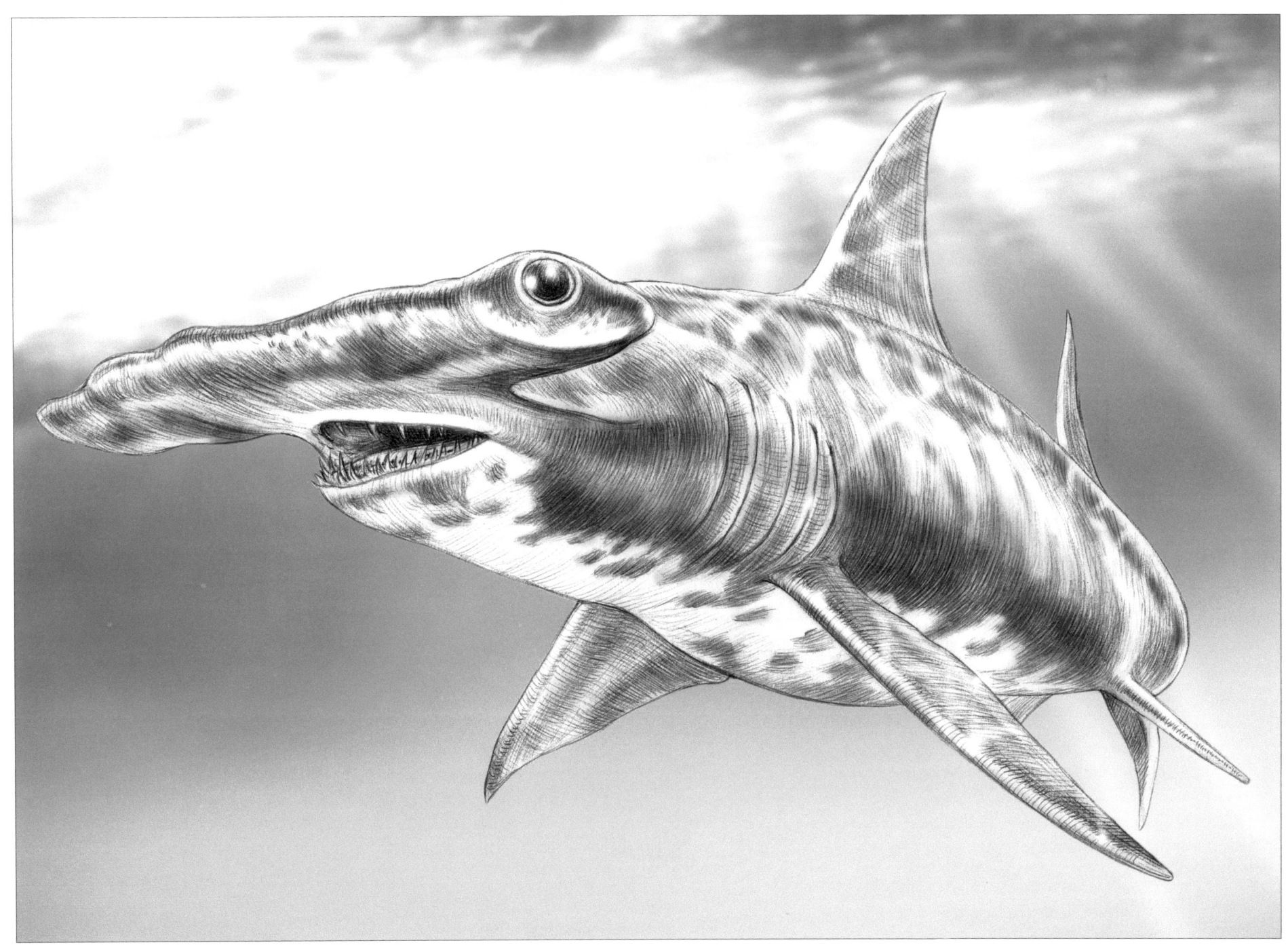
Great Hammerhead Shark

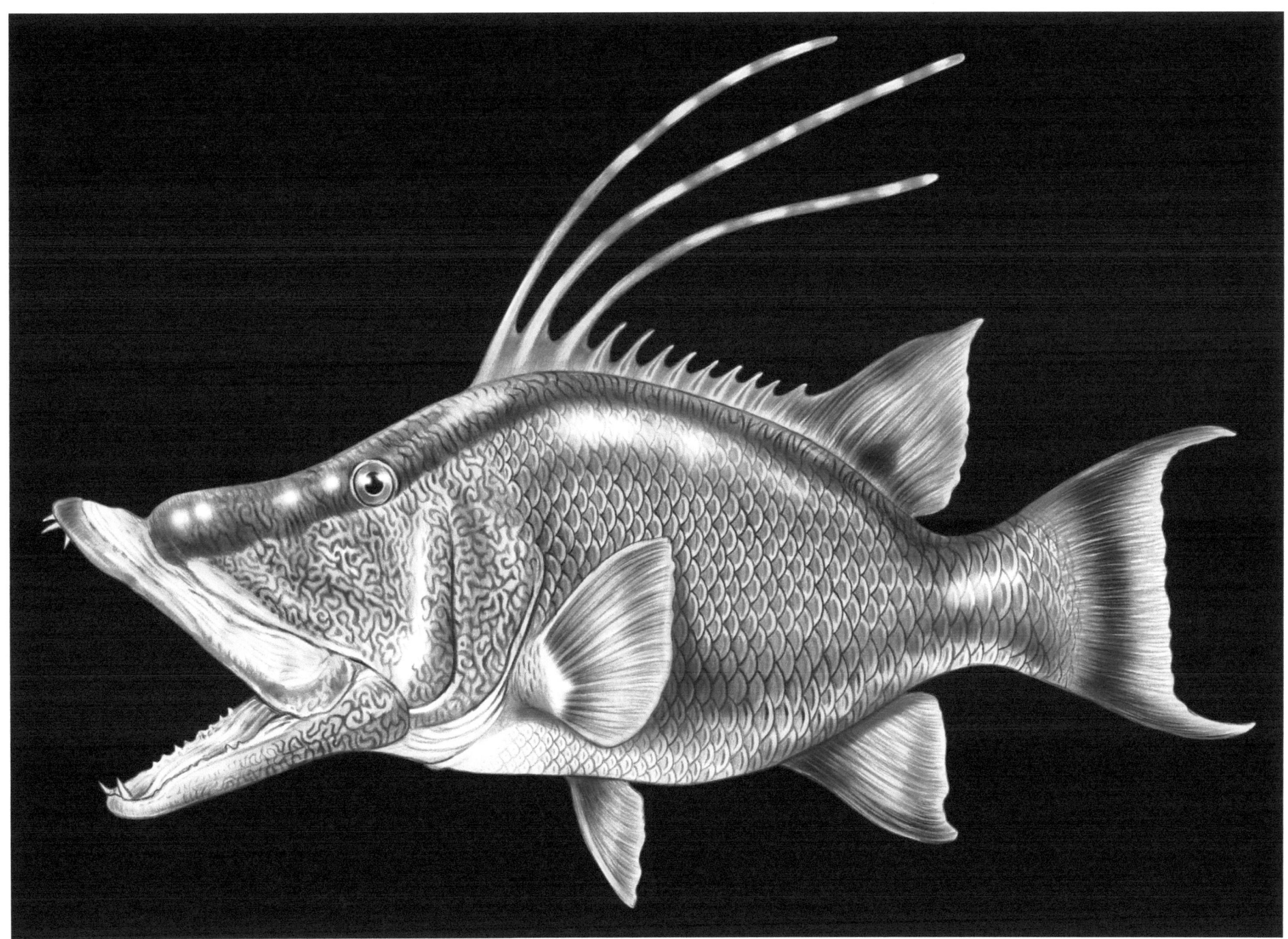

Hogfish

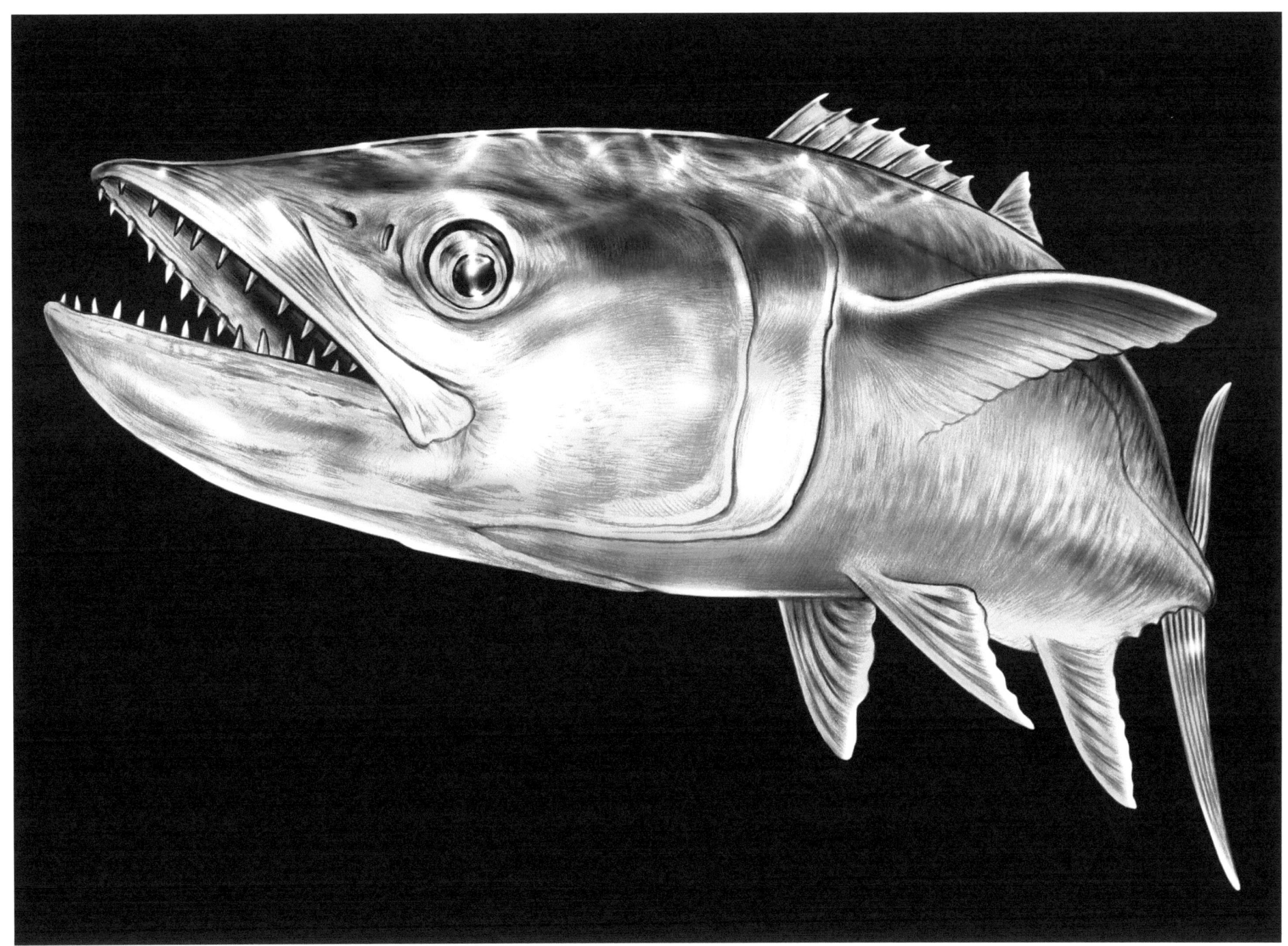

King Mackerel

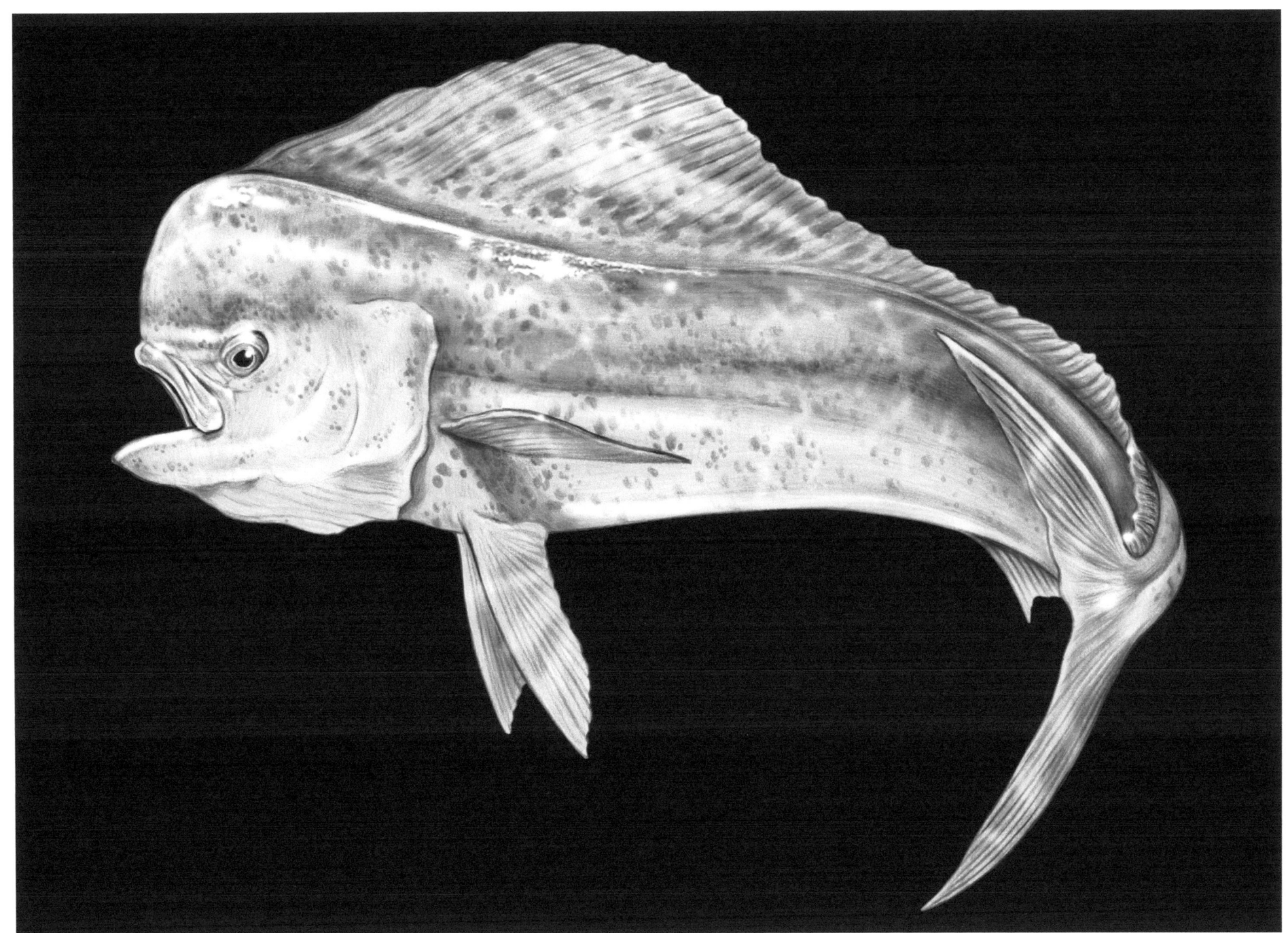

Mahi Mahi

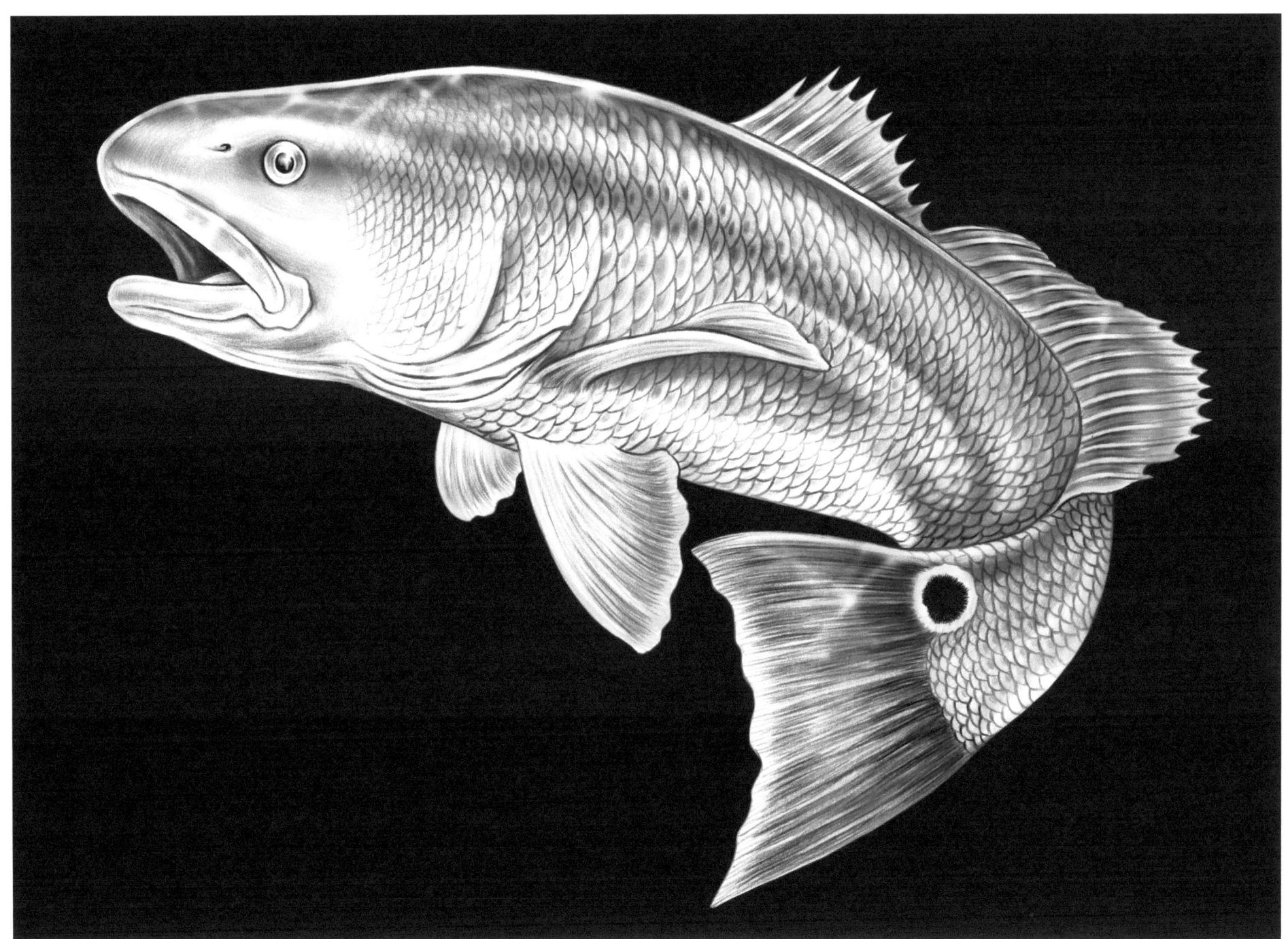

Red Drum

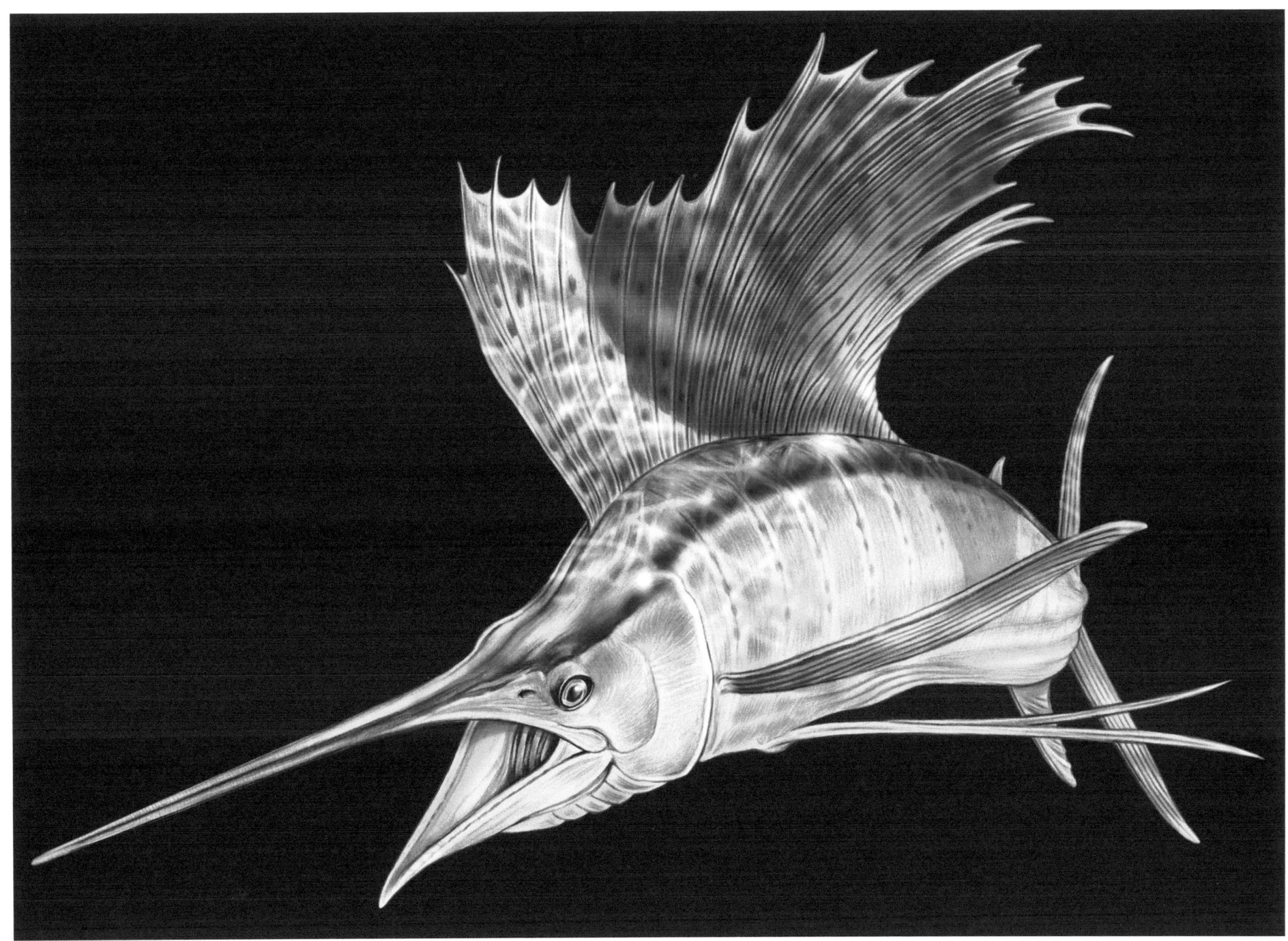

Sailfish

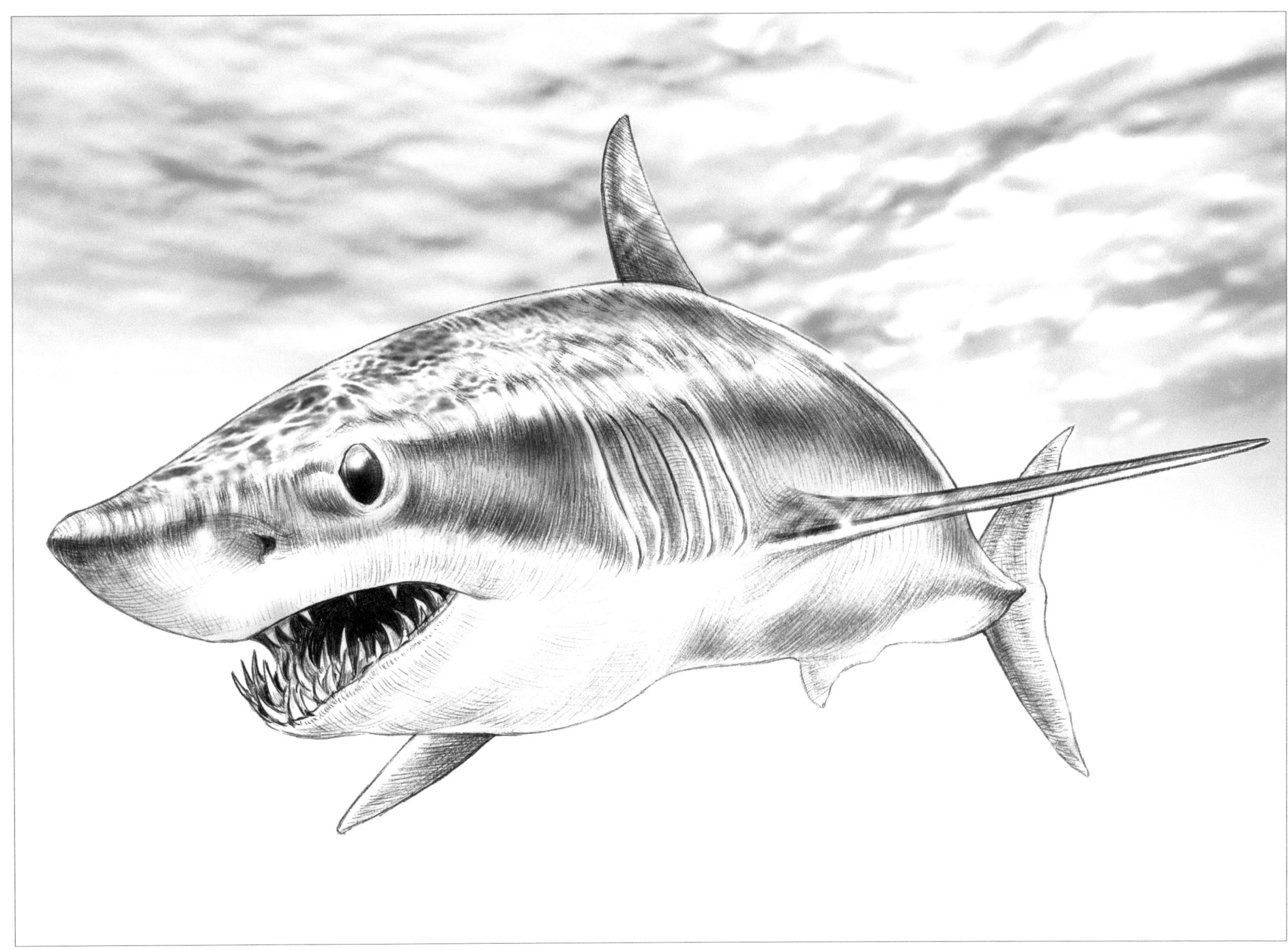

Shortfin Mako Shark

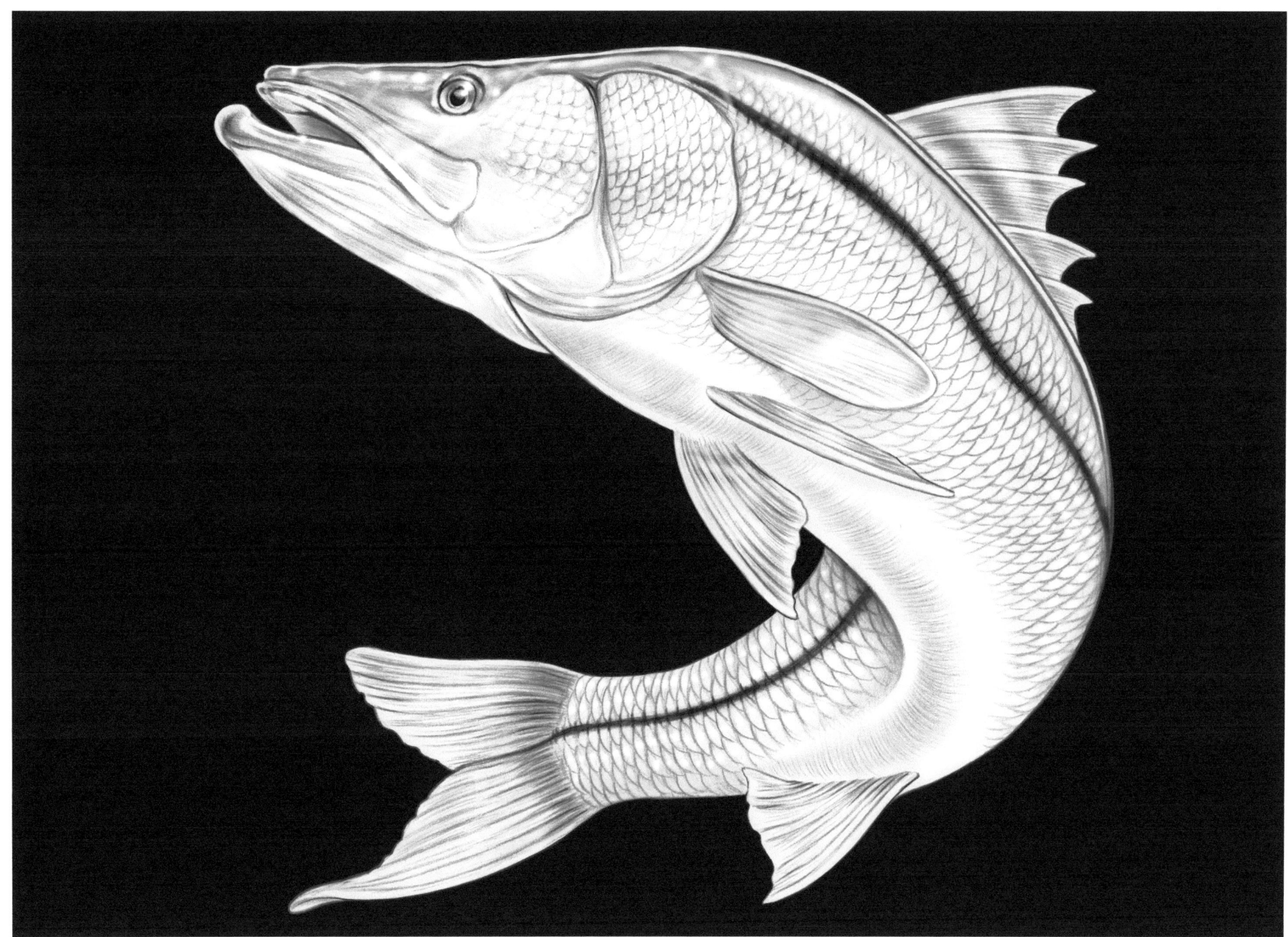
Snook

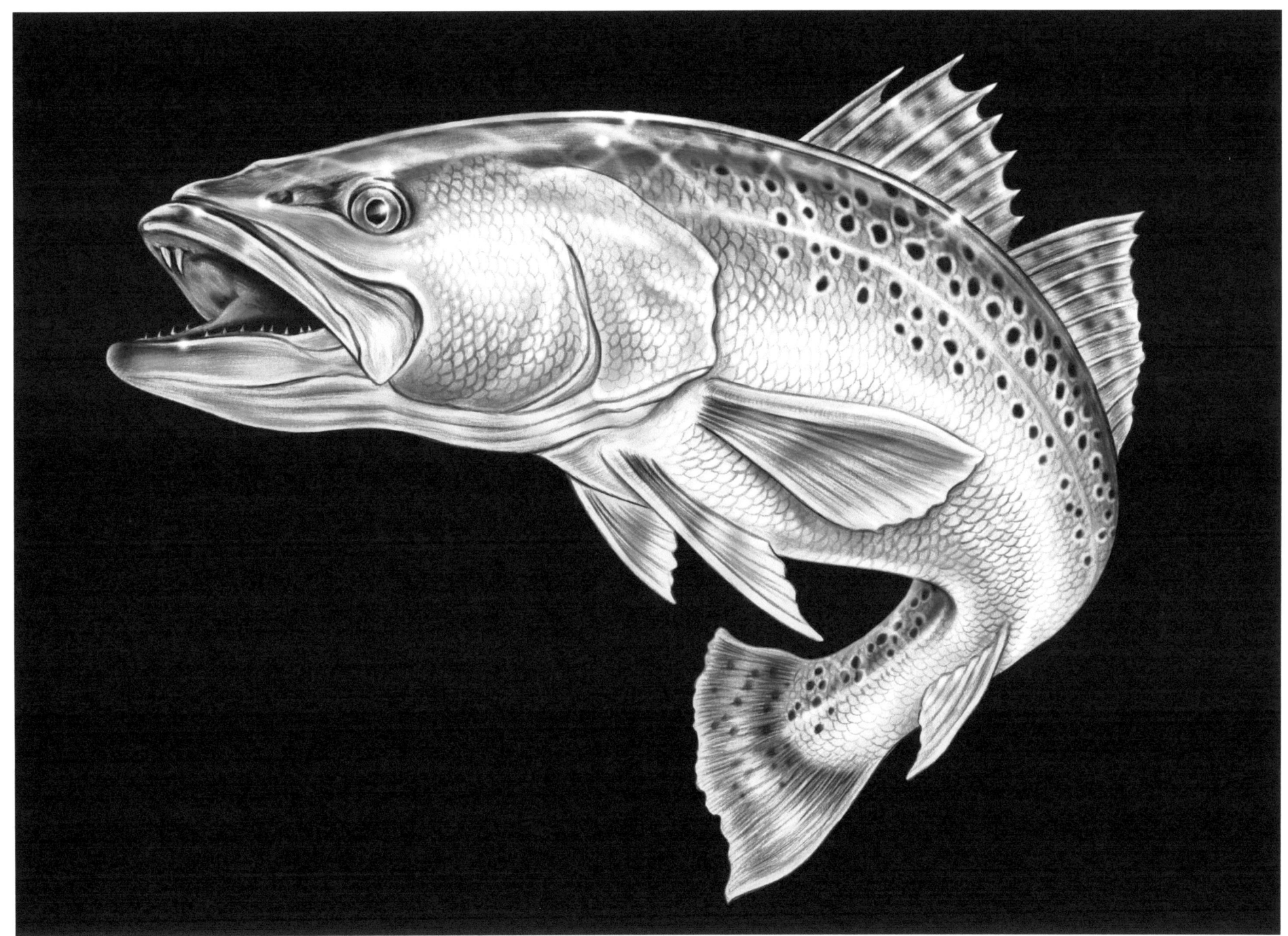
Speckled Trout

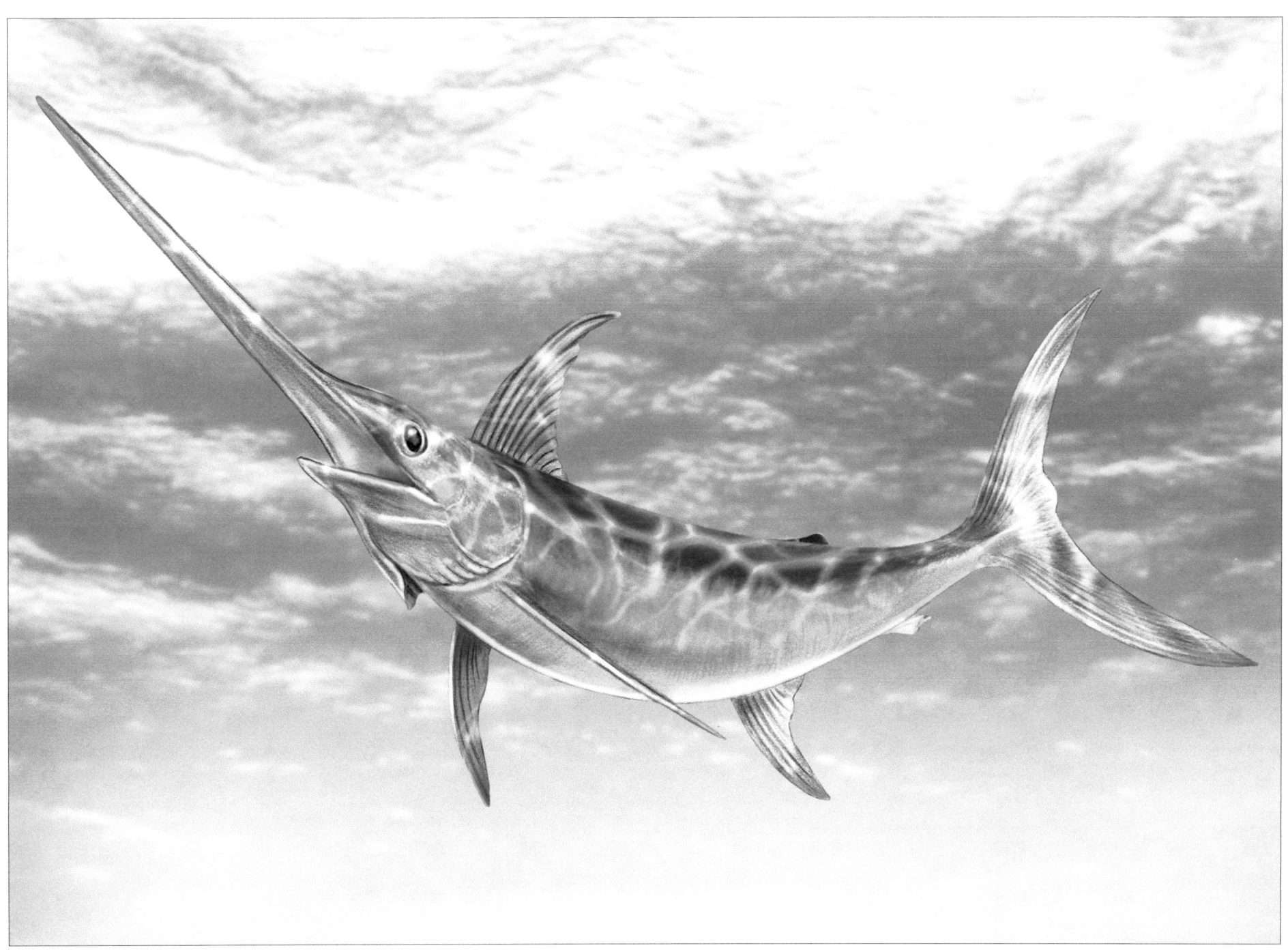

Swordfish

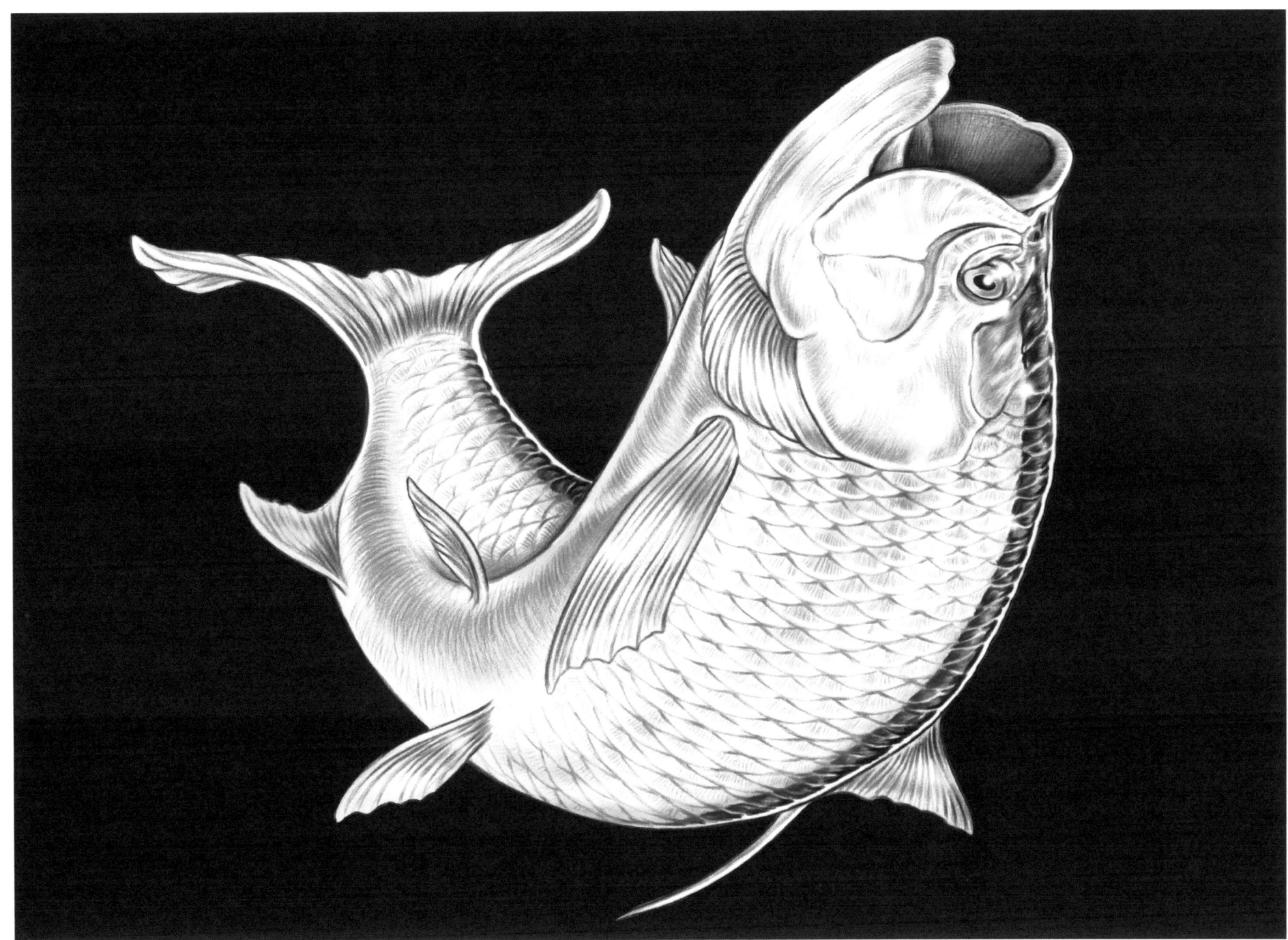

Tarpon

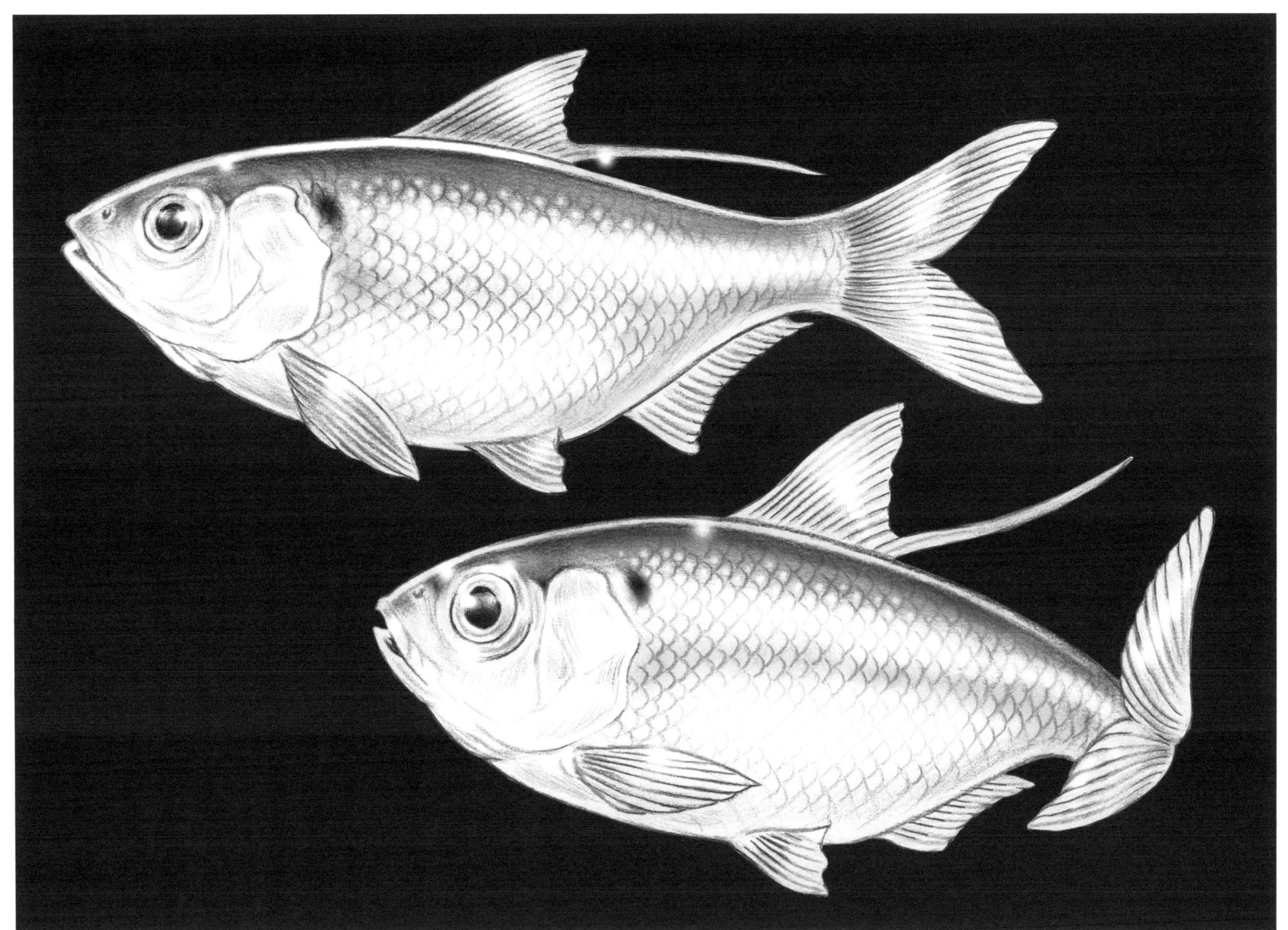

Threadfin Shad

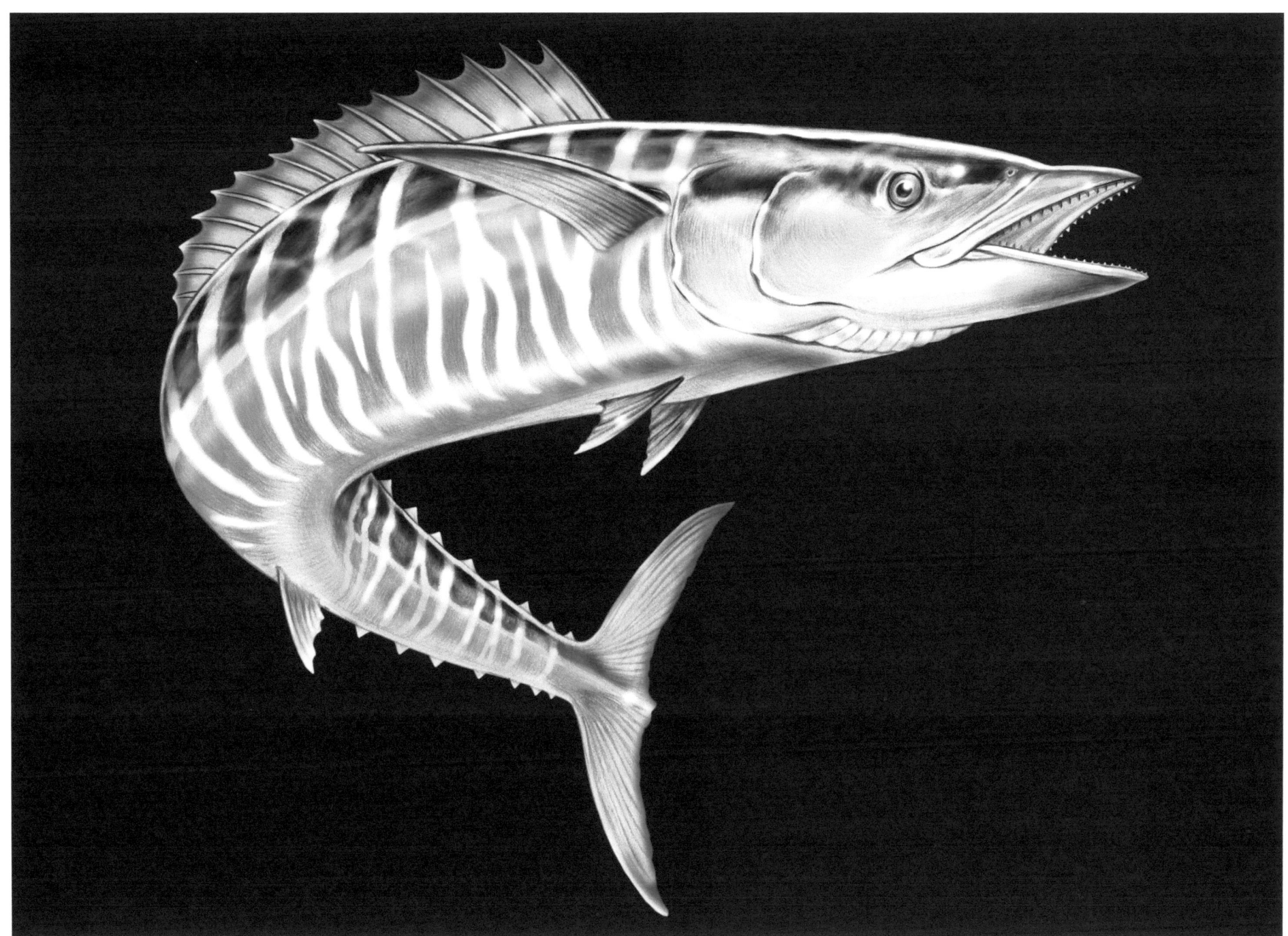
Wahoo

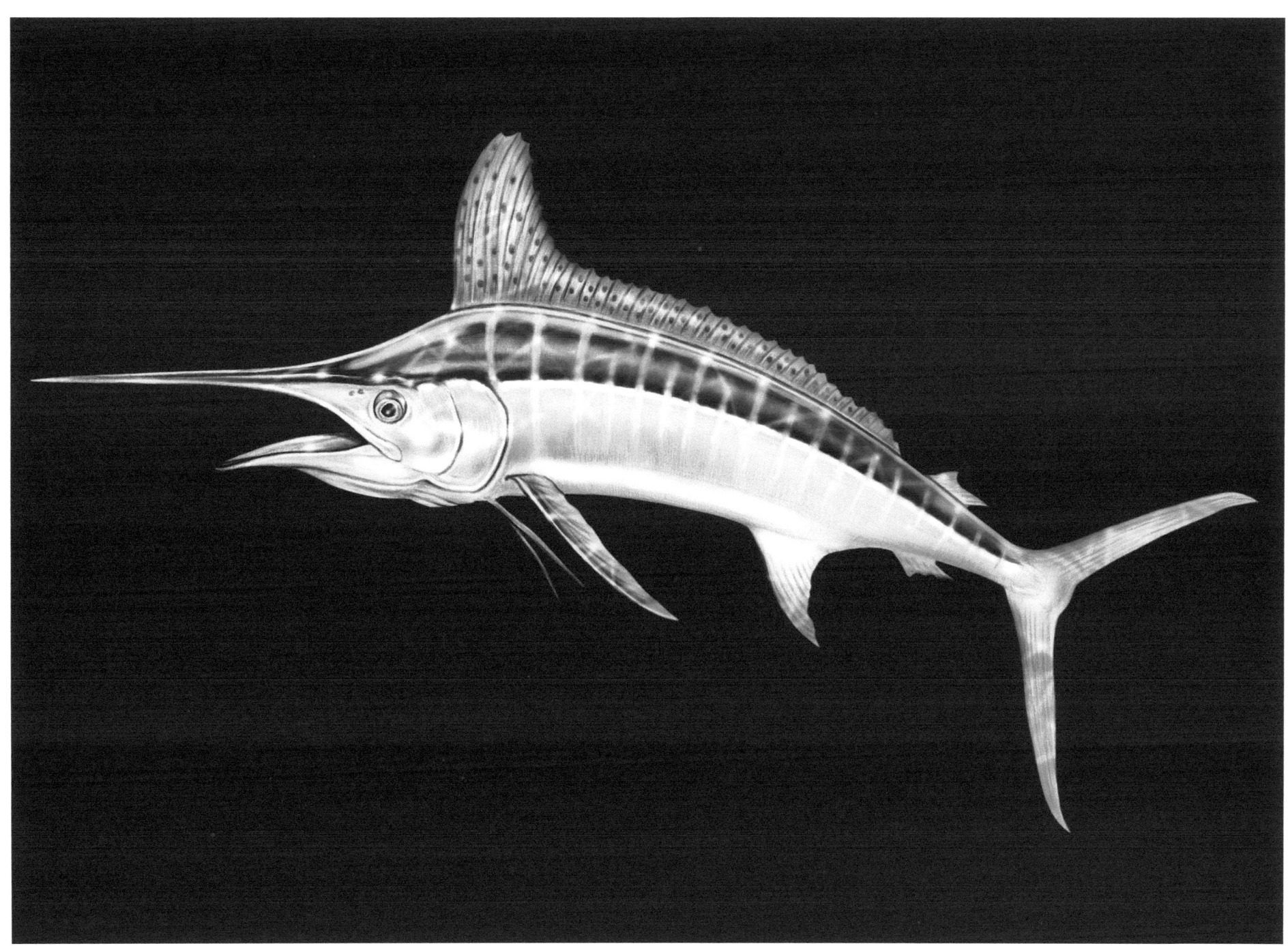
White Marlin

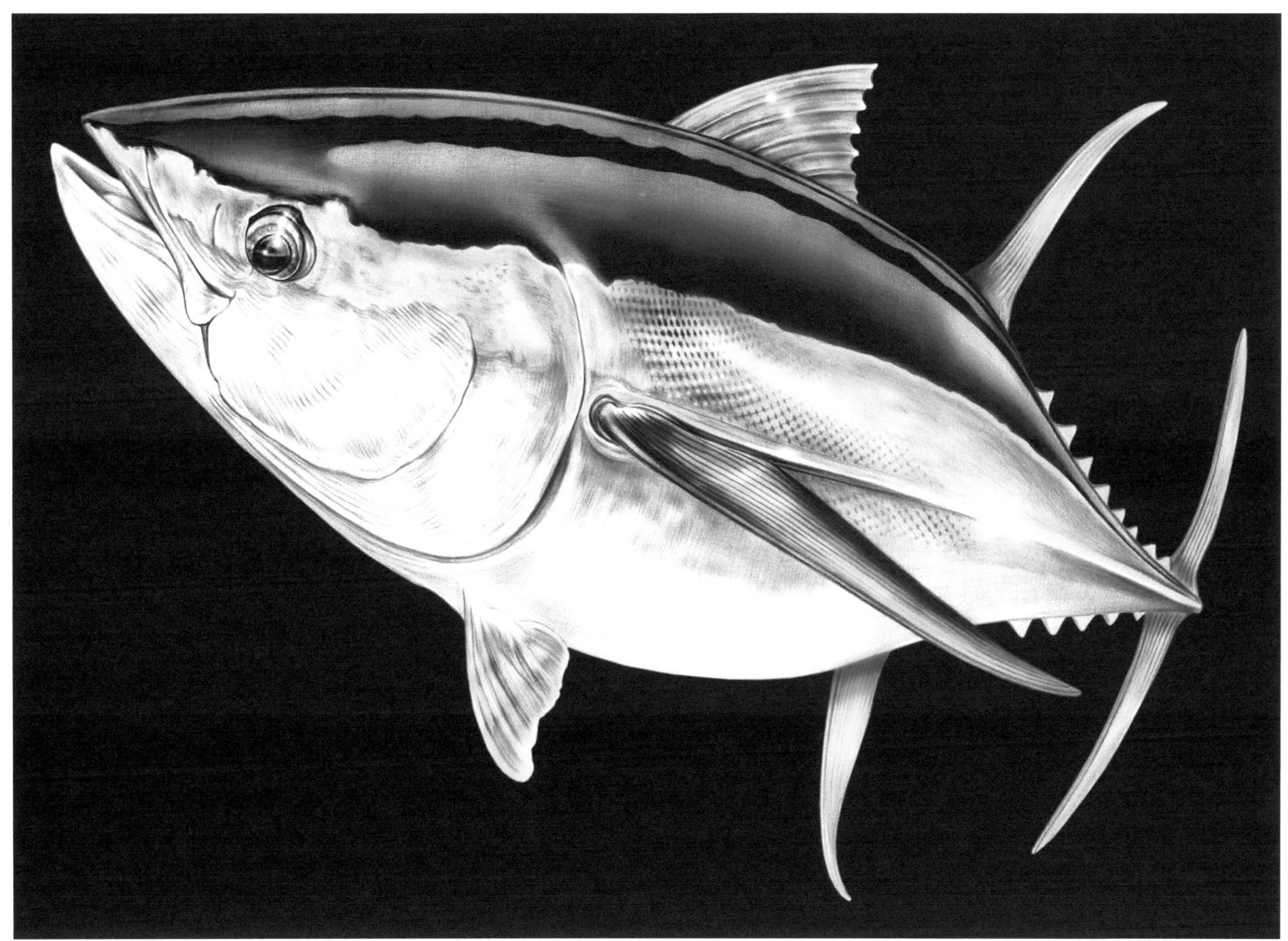
Yellowfin Tuna

**Tim Jeffs** is a New York City based artist and illustrator who has been creating dynamic artwork for over 25 years. Animals are a favorite subject matter of his, along with the complex and intricate details these creatures possess. *"The incredible diversity and complexity of animals has always intrigued me. They offer endless pleasure to look and marvel upon. In every drawing I try to capture the unique quality of each particular animal. I hope you enjoy my perspective, love and admiration of these incredible creatures."*

Visit my website for prints, digital coloring books and coloring lessons:

## www.TimJeffsArt.com

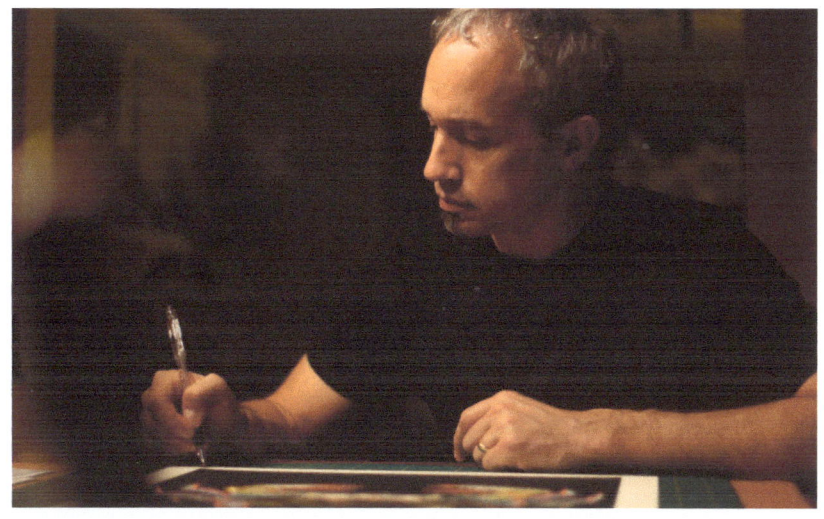

# Discover the full line of Tim Jeffs' Published Coloring Books

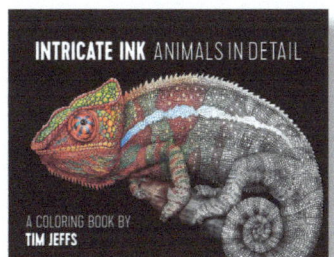
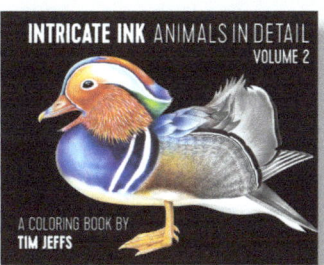
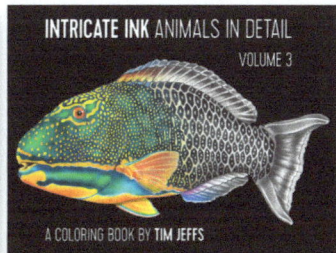
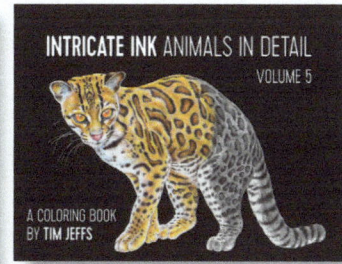
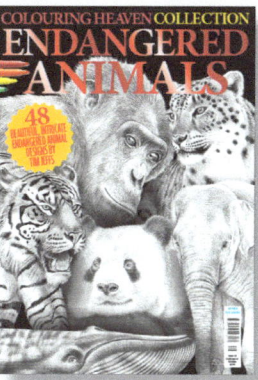
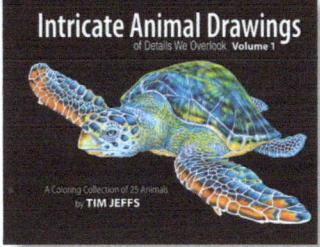
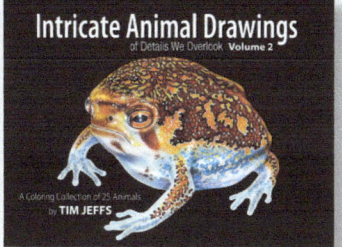

**Intricate Ink Animals In Detail Volume 1, 2 3 and 5, and Intricate Animal Drawings Volume 1 and 2 are available at:**
Amazon.com
Bookdepository.com

**Colouring Heaven Collection Endangered Animals**
Available at: Colouringheaven.com

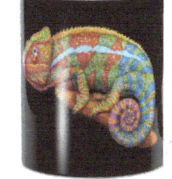

# Discover Tim Jeffs' Merchandise

**Etsy Shop**
www.etsy.com/shop/TimJeffsArt

**Society6 Shop**
www.society6.com/TimJeffsArt

**Redbubble Shop**
TimJeffsArt.redbubble.com

**TeePublic Shop**
https://www.teepublic.com/user/tim-jeffs-art

# Discover the full line of Tim Jeffs Digital Coloring Books and Lessons at www.timjeffsart.com

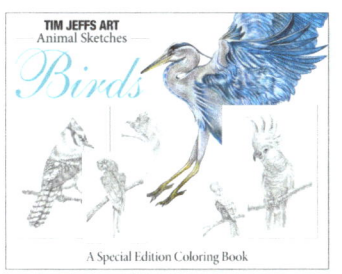 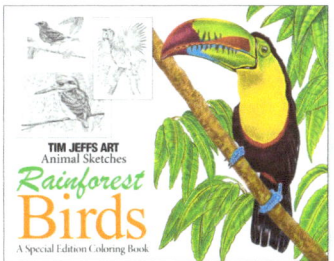 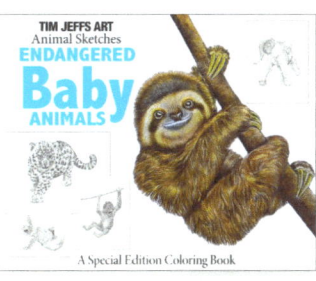 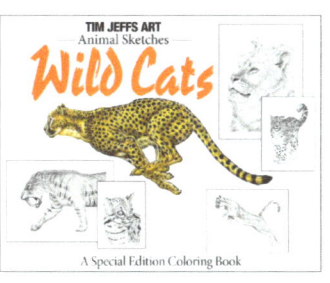 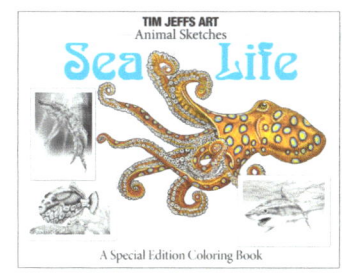
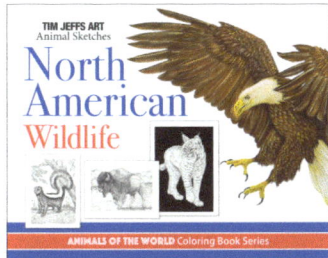 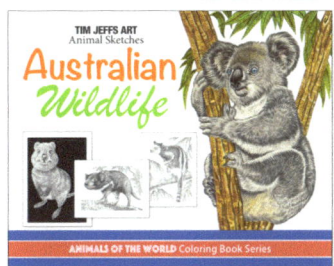 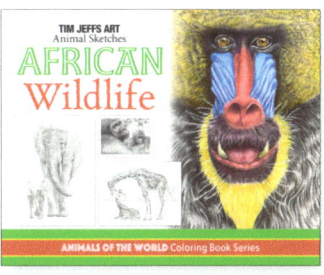 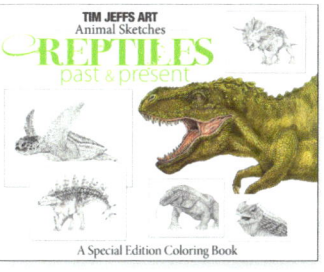 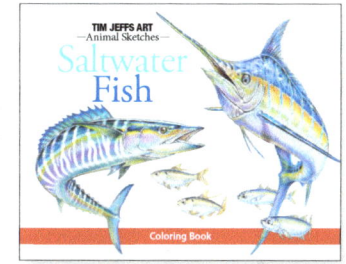
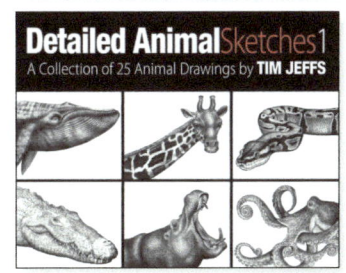 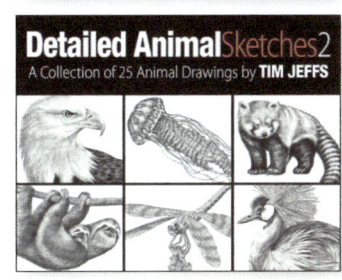 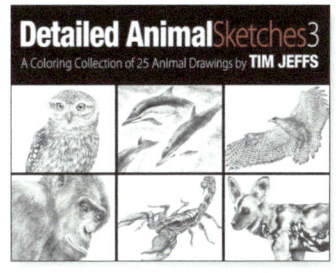 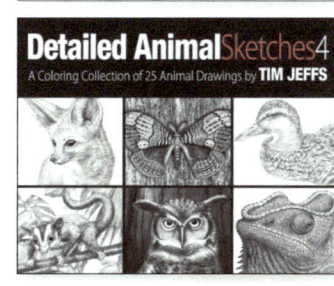 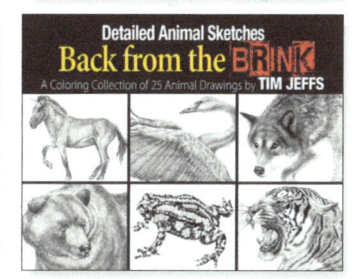
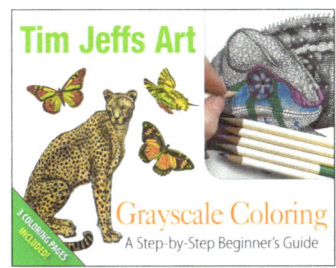 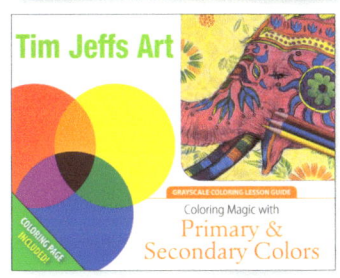 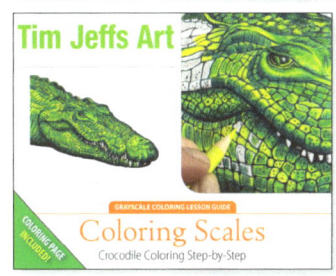 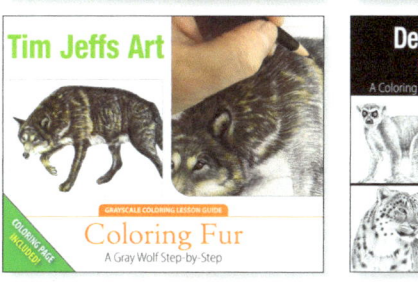 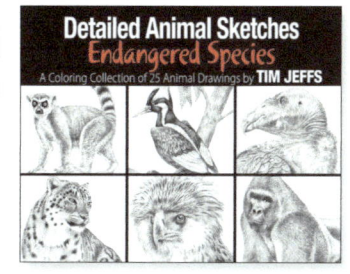
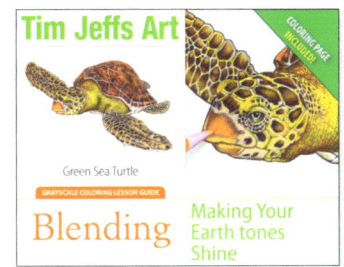 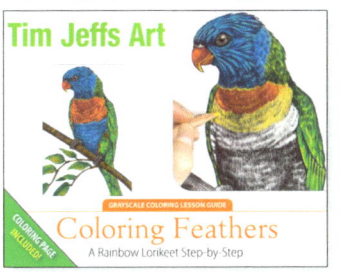 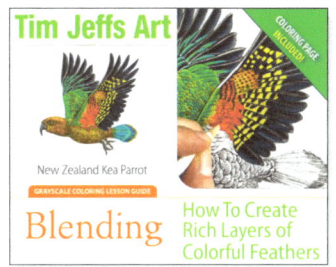 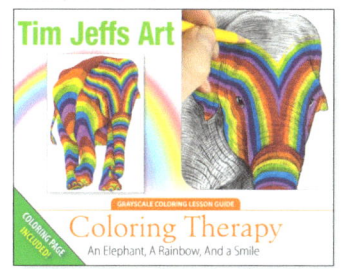 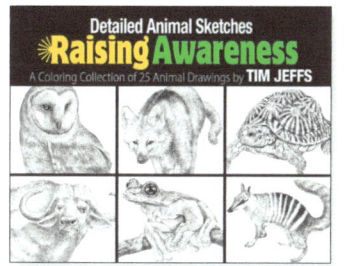

# TIM JEFFS ART  Online Resources

## Share Your Creativity with the World!

Join the ever-expanding coloring group of animal lovers who inspire each other through their colorings of the animals from Tim's books and lessons. With thousands of members from all around the world, Tim's Facebook group "Intricate Ink Coloring Group" is a creative and safe space where everyone is welcome. Jo Warren, the groups all-inspiring administrator will welcome you in with open arms and is there to encourage everyone to just have fun no matter your coloring skill level. Come join, we can't wait to have you as a member! Join Tim's Facebook Coloring Group at:

**www.facebook.com/groups/intricateink**

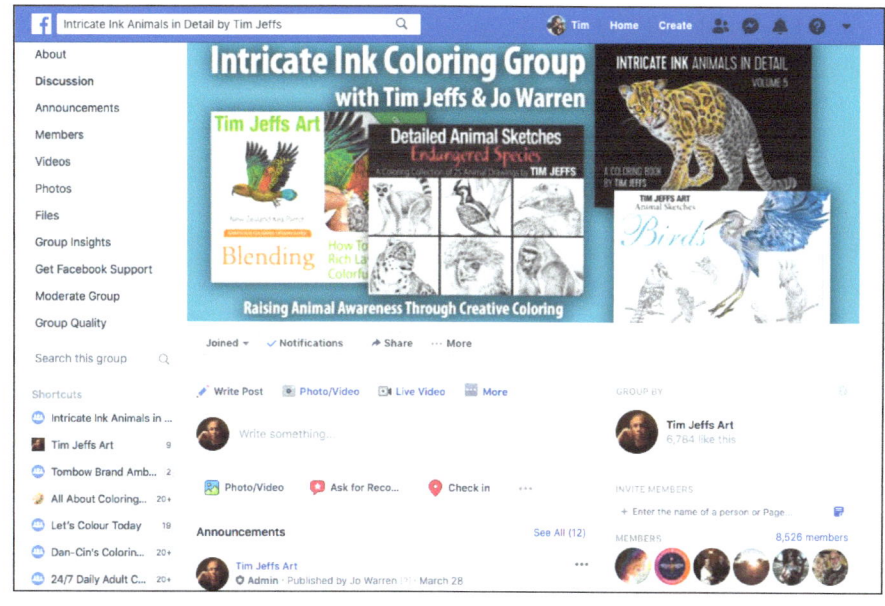

## Visit the Home of Tim Jeffs Art

**TimJeffsArt.com** is my home on the web where I display all of my work and various projects. I hope you can stop by for a visit! You'll find my new shop where signed and unsigned prints of all of my animal drawings are available to purchase, along with the complete library of my digital download coloring books and grayscale coloring lessons. In the conservation section, you can see the projects that I am very proud of. Using my art to preserve wildlife is so important to me.

**www.TimJeffsArt.com**

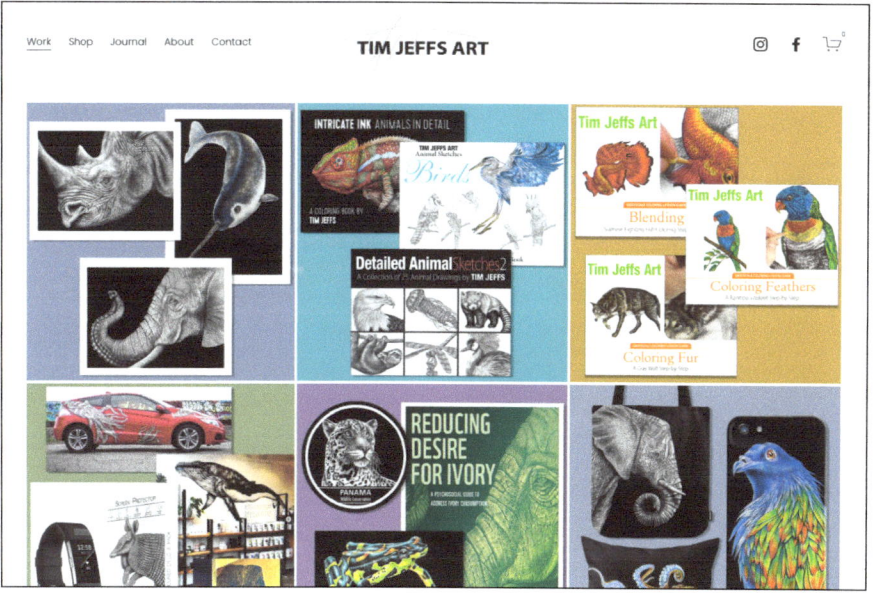

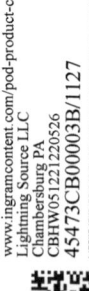